Usborne

Art Deco
patterns
to
color

Illustrated by Mary Kilvert
Designed by Emily Beevers
Written by Emily Bone

Art deco patterns

Art deco is a design style made up of angular and curved shapes that became popular during the 1920s. In the early 20th century, many artists and designers used elements of art deco in their work.

A new style

From art and architecture to fashion and tableware, art deco affected all forms of design.

Flowers, animals and other things from nature were simplified. Art deco patterns had repeated shapes and all kinds of bold, contrasting colors.

Black provided a stark contrast to bright colors.

Flowers, like these poppies, were given simple outlines.

A pattern of flying seagulls

This was a 'sunburst', a popular art deco pattern that looked like rays of sunshine.

Day to day

Art deco vases, tea sets, glasswear and other everyday objects brought deco design into peoples' homes. Things were made in surprising shapes and were covered in colorful patterns.

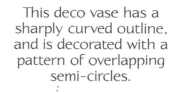

This deco vase has a sharply curved outline, and is decorated with a pattern of overlapping semi-circles.

Fashion

Fashion designers were inspired by art deco shapes and patterns. Dresses and overcoats were designed with sharp lines and fabric was printed with art deco patterns. Jewelry was big and bold.

The fringing of this dress from 1925 is cut into a curved pattern.

Bold buildings

Buildings had striking designs too, like this spire from the Chrysler building in New York. It's designed as a sunburst with triangular windows that sparkle when they catch the sunlight.

Deco advertisements

Advertisements from the deco period were designed in a flat, yet decorative, style. Pictures like these would have appeared in fashion magazines.

Vacation resorts commissioned artists to create eye-catching posters with bold and distinctive type.

SKI EN CRANS

Fashion show

Fashion designers experimented with simple, clean lines and repeated art deco patterns and colors. Here are some examples of deco-style outfits.

Big, bold flower patterns were popular.

Use alternate bright colors with black to fill in the patterns on this dress.

Art deco parasol

The colors of the stripes on this coat should match the striped hat.

Dressing table

Even small things were given the art deco treatment. You might have found these on a 1920s dressing table.

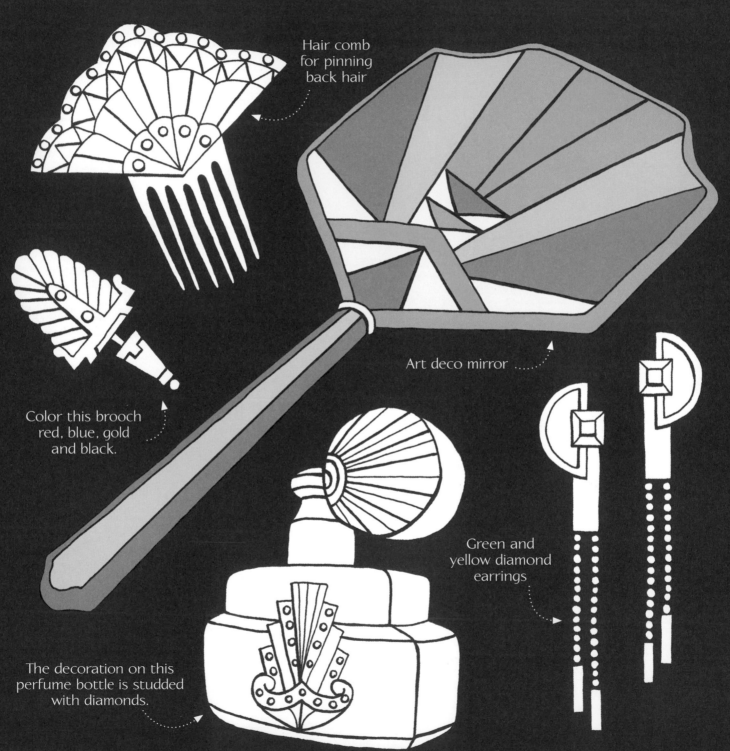

Hair comb for pinning back hair

Art deco mirror

Color this brooch red, blue, gold and black.

Green and yellow diamond earrings

The decoration on this perfume bottle is studded with diamonds.

Necklace with rectangular glass and plastic beads

Perfume bottle made from colored glass

Face powder compact

Butterfly earrings

Black, gold and silver link bracelet

Fashionable fans

Fans were fashionable accessories. They were often decorated with striking patterns, like these.

Time for tea

In fashionable tea rooms, people were served afternoon tea in art deco sets. As well as being decorated with patterns, the outlines of cups, pitchers and sugar bowls reflected the curved and angular art deco style. Designers became known for their art deco pottery.

Try to match the rest of the tea set to the colors on this plate.

This milk jug has an interesting mix of different patterns – sunburst and flowers.

These tea cups have sharp, triangular handles.

In the city

The first skyscrapers were built in the 1930s. They had gleaming, deco-style spires. Some buildings had curved walls painted with different patterns.

Glamorous glass

Some art deco buildings were designed with stunning, stained glass windows. This window has a sunburst pattern.

Oriental patterns

Many designers were inspired by patterns used in traditional Asian and African art. Here are art deco versions of ancient Japanese textile designs.

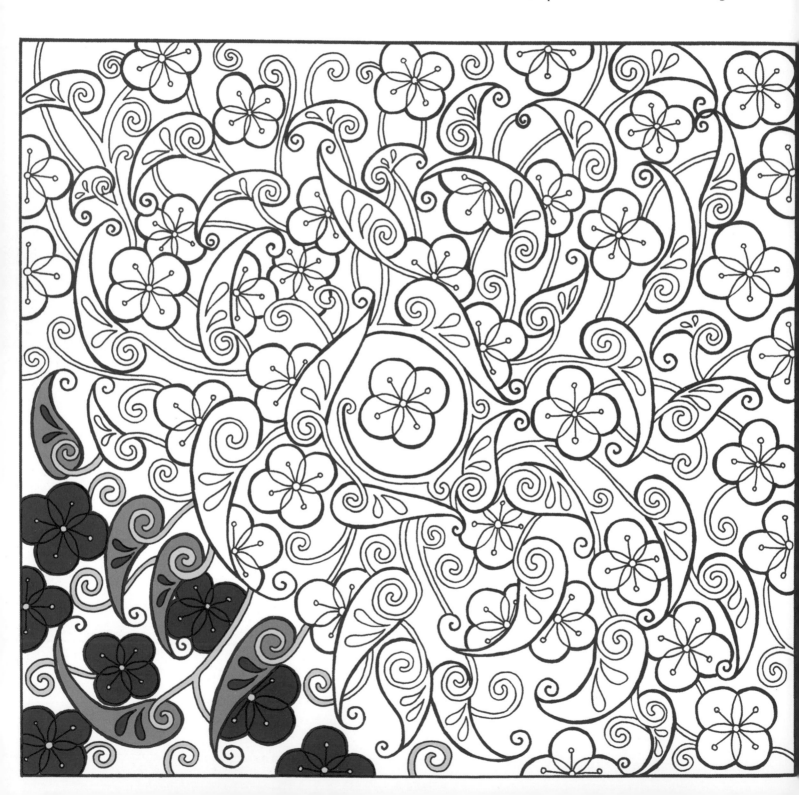

On stage

Dazzling art deco costumes and stage designs added
to the spectacle of ballets and musicals.

Art deco patterns

All the patterns on the next few pages are based on art deco designs taken from fabrics, buildings and interiors.

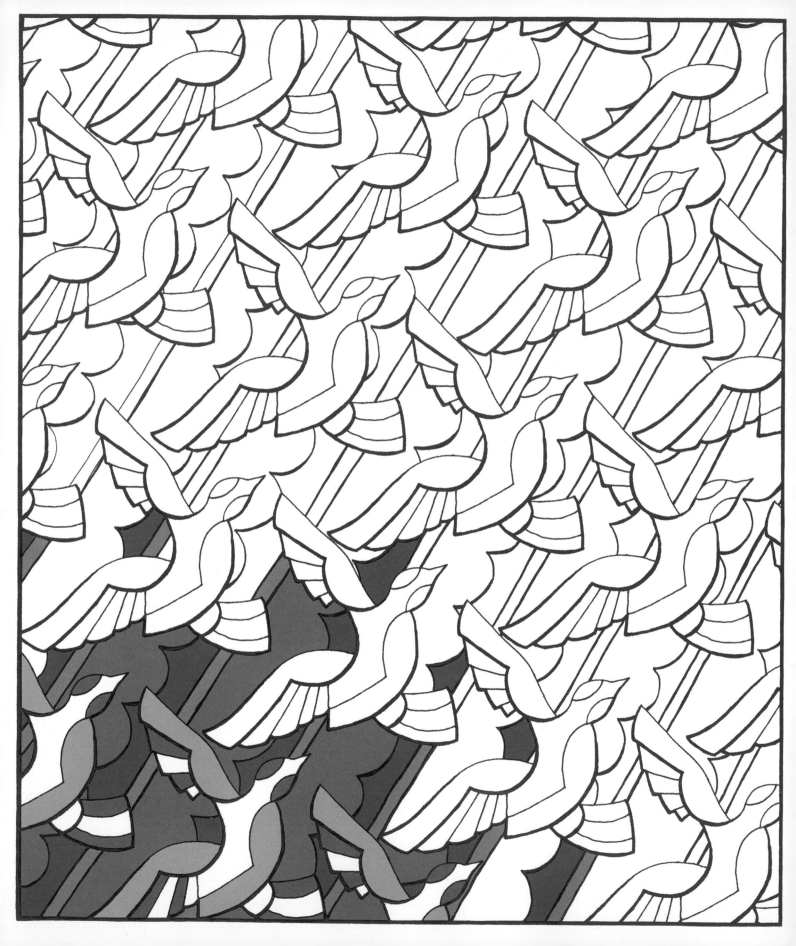

First published in 2013 by Usborne Publishing Ltd, Usborne House, 83-85 Saffron Hill, London ECIN 8RT, England. www.usborne.com